Naomi Foyle

The Night Pavilion

First published in 2008
by Waterloo Press (Hove)
126 Furze Croft
Furze Hill
Hove BN3 1PF

Printed in Palatino 11pt by
One Digital
54 Hollingdean Road
East Sussex BN2 4AA

Cover image and author photo © John Luke Chapman 2008
Typesetting by Matilda Persson

Naomi Foyle is hereby identified as author of this
work in accordance with Section 77 of the Copyright,
Designs and Patents Act 1988

A CIP record for this book is available
from the British Library

ISBN 978-1-906742-05-8

For Carla Jacob
in memory of our London Season

By the same author

Canada (Echo Room Press, 2005)
Red Hot & Bothered (Lansdowne Press, 2003)
Febrifugue (Treeplantsink Press, 1996)

Hush: An Opera In Two Bestial Acts
(Theatre Passe Muraille, Toronto, 1990)

Acknowledgements

Thanks are due to the editors of the following publications:

Ambit, The Big Spoon, Bonjour Brighton, The Gown Literary Supplement, The London Magazine, My Mother Threw Knives, Poetry London, PN Review, Red Hot & Bothered (Lansdowne Press, 2003), *The Rialto, Shout!* (Greece), *The Slab, The Stony Thursday Book* (Ireland), *Tears In The Fence, Trivia* (USA).

A version of *Aphrodite's Answering Machine* was recorded as a spoken word CD, set to music by Richard Miles (2002). 'On The Acropolis' was set in a lightbox by Jim McKevitt, and exhibited at Queen's Studio Belfast (2002). 'Good Definition' was produced as a videopoem by Anneliese Holles, and won the Hastings Word On The Street Festival film poem competition (2004). 'Portrait of The Snow Queen as a Young Bitch' is a character study for a libretto based on the Hans Christian Andersen story, a work-in-progress with composer Nadja Gabriela Plein. Some verses of 'The Ballad of The Broken Hearted' have been set to music by Paul van Gelder and The Tipsy Gypsies, and recorded under the title 'No Man's Land' (2007).

In addition to my collaborators, I would like to thank all those who have critiqued or otherwise encouraged these poems, in particular Graham Ackroyd, Maude Casey, John Luke Chapman, Brendan Cleary, John Davies, Hugh Dunkerley, Sarah Hymas, Simon Jenner, Catherine Lupton, Kai Merriott, John O'Donoghue, Louise Reiser, Bethan Roberts, David Swann, Lorna Thorpe and Bernard Selinger. I am also grateful to Arts Council England for funding me to edit this book with the assistance of Stephen Knight, who became a highly valued mentor of my poetry during my MA at Goldsmiths College.

I thank Paul van Gelder and my family, Mary Griffiths, Rebecca Riches and Stefan Riches for their loving faith in me. Finally, I wish to honour two guiding spirits: Mairtín Crawford and my late mother, Brenda Macdonald Riches. Without whom, and always with me.

Contents

Darkroom Debutantes

Buddleia In Bloom	17
Frau Dittmer's Divorce	18
A Study In Moonlight	20
Uncommon Prayer	21
In The Heat Of The Moment	22
Mademoiselle Mal Chance	23
On The Acropolis	24
Sylvia Plath (ps)	25
Portrait of the Snow Queen as a Young Bitch	26
The Riddle Ground	28
The Dance	30
Monster	33
A Pint, A Drop Or A Rope	34
Bonjour Nouvel An	35
Future Tense	36
Midnight Versions of Anna Akhmatova	37

Aphrodite's Answering Machine

Liberties	41
Good Definition	42
Crop Circles	44
For Achilleas: Because I Wouldn't Let Him Watch	46
Not Quite Arrived	48

The Night Pavilion

Misremembering the Night	53
Vanitas	54
Animal, Vegetable, Mineral	55
The Ballad of the Broken-Hearted	56
Cruella Degenerates	58
The Angel of Anarchy	59

Duet   60
Natasha   61
Miss Dickinson Regrets   64
Boas & Blindfolds   65
Your Summer Arm   67
Small Blossoms   68
Things I'm Cool With Now   69

Notes

Essential Oils — are wrung —
The Attar from the Rose
Be not expressed by Suns — alone —
It is the gift of Screws —
Emily Dickinson

Darkroom Debutantes

Buddleia In Bloom

Lilac, powder blue, magenta,
pendulous and preening,
their airy beauty undisputed,
these teenage witches at the ball
exude an almost rodent charm.
In shapely tapered gowns
they strain to catch the faintest scent
of humans drawing near.

The butterflies are dance cards:
write your name on golden wings,
then lean close to your partner
and let her half-tumescent snout
insert its spell of tiny petals
inside your unprotected ear.

Frau Dittmer's Divorce
after *Luck* by Gert Hofmann

I was just a girl from Dortmund —
I knew nothing about Thomas Mann.
I thought poetry was romantic,
but I didn't expect to have to eat it
for breakfast, lunch and tea.
Ach, it's dreadful to admit
your mother was right
about the one time in your life
you disobeyed her,
but I understand utterly now
her refusal to come to the wedding.
She could see right through
his murky green eyes —
but to me they glimmered like jewels.
I was just a secretary then,
he was so handsome,
and I didn't imagine I could ever do better
than a writer on a private income,
that's what he said he was.
A writer on a private income
needs a pretty Frau, he'd say,
and two plump children,
so he can walk along the Rhine
and hold his head up
amongst all the people of the world.
Otherwise its purgatory,
candle stubs, and old men
with tobacco-stained fingers
for company ...
is that the fate
you want for me,
my little sweet strudel?
he'd ask. Then he'd tickle me
with his moustaches
and I would stroke his fine waistcoat

and murmur,
'Of course not,
no.'

Well, I gave him
two fat children
so he could fill their heads with tripe.
And I worked and worked
for Herr Herkanrath,
so he could spend all day in his study
writing his novel
and reading that wrinkled postcard
from the 'godlike' Thomas Mann.
And he kept telling me
The Magic Table
needed just one more leg
before we could all sit round it
and toast the writer and his life.
Well, I tell you,
we had to burn *The Magic Table*
last winter for heat
and if Herr Herkanrath
hadn't lent us that money
I don't know what we would have done.
Children need boots
and hats and schoolbooks,
not nonsense about windows and villains
and the 'duplicitous nature of time'.
And a woman, a woman needs dresses
and carpets and trips on a boat
to an island of linden trees
where Herr Herkanrath asked me to marry him
and I said 'Yes,
oh yes
I will, and my mother will
bake the cake
and my father
will shake
your firm hand.'

A Study in Moonlight

The bookshelf lies in wait,
baring rows of spiny teeth.
I'm the little bird
who cleans its grinning gums —
if I sometimes nick a bit of prose
I am a tolerated thief.

The armchair wallows in the corner,
a bulging hippo's head,
ominously burping
when I try to sit and read.
To save my skin, I feed it
the foliage of my clothes.

A mean gorilla mama,
the bureau grinds her fists into the floor.
Clinging to her chest,
I'm a hairless, cuckoo child:
tugging at her metal nipples,
rooting in her jaws

for the tender tips of words.

Uncommon Prayer

Lord, save me from the light:

The sordid nickel glitter
            of the high street,
The pale and milky veil
        through which lovers drain the night,
The blatant afternoon
        that blares our flaws up to the sun,
The golden syrup of July
            making fly strips of the young.

Make the summers short,
Oh Lord, please
Make the evenings long.

Give me the pool of lamp glow
                to bathe my weary bones,
Provide a starless soup of cloud
            to drown the fickle moon,
Give me the flicker of the candle
                to tickle and to pique,
And the dimmer switch to finger
            as I rehearse my blue mystique.

Let me close my eyes, oh Lord,
Please invite the darkness in.
Let me glimmer like a sequin
Lost within your black sheepskin.

In The Heat
Of The Moment

The sun pours itself
into bright

golden bowls,
drops them

all over your lawn.
Like the fly

at the heart
of the buttercup,

I wash my hands
in the light

of one
thin-stemmed flower –

rubbing & rubbing
two sticks together,

as if clean,
they might break

into flame.

Mademoiselle Mal Chance

A secret of eyelashes;
    a daisy dipped in pitch;
      a delicate brooch
pinned to the side of the tub —

        until I approach
with my plundering streams,
my inveigling finger:
a menace,
      a moment,
          a flood.

Where is your fine lifeline, spider?
Where are your eight water wings?
You sprawl, a legless gamine.

I share a hot bath with your corpse.
It clings to my skin like a mole.
My mascara runs in the steam.

On the Acropolis

I watch the bee abandon power of flight,
pull his bud to earth with weight
  made faint by fumes
   as strong as gasoline.
The bush is bright, a bomb
  of warm, potential tombs.

But no, he won't surrender to his swoon.
Nectar bursts and sprays
  like dictates of the Queen:
she waits inside the hive, her harvest
  hissing moon —
a burr of blithe obedience, he licks
  the blossom clean.

Sylvia Plath (ps)

I admire her
          stubborn efforts
to find a rhyme for orange:
  her singed lozenges
                    of light
nibble at the edges
          of my tongue —
    the pithy muscle stiffens:
an arrowhead,
          a grapefruit spoon,
  smeared
      with sour blancmange.

Portrait of the Snow Queen as a Young Bitch

Glissandos of snow were in vogue that year:
frigid crystals deflowered my earlobes.
For a colourless fashion that would never last,
I frosted the tips of my breasts,
scattered a fortune on see-through robes
trimmed with the bellies of deer.

My step-sister wore a hoar-lamé gown.
She tinkled in icicle heels.
But her cheeks turned pink as French roast beef
when Lord Sheffield pirouetted his knife.
He gave her a cape cut from two baby seals
and my forehead composed a new frown.

I was the girl with skate-blade hips,
born in a paperweight storm.
As Mother skied into a coke overdose
and Father blockaded the Swiss,
I learned how to press my skeletal form
into the absence of lips.

Wife Number Two was a honeycombed slut
melting in front of the fire.
Now Father stayed in from winter to spring;
and the governess taught me to sing.
My sister and I made a pitch-perfect choir —
as long as she kept her mouth shut.

I didn't desire Lord Sheffield to love me:
he was ruddy and coarse as a bullock.
But I was the eldest and custom required
he court me until I got bored.
Antarctica howled and creaked in my stomach
when he lifted my sister above me.

In winter, the Earth submits to a law
of cold and majestic returns:
flowers that blossom and blush in the summer
succumb to an enemy glamour.
Scoring the chords of my 'Wedding Nocturnes'
I carved a new front in the war.

Deep in the palace, my mother's harmonium
was gathering shadows and dust.
Composition in hand, I demanded that Father
relinquish the key to the chamber.
Alone with my heirloom, I scrubbed at the rust
till the metal reeds shone like plutonium.

Wielding a blowtorch, a miniature fork-lift,
and a textbook on sound engineering,
I soldered a dog whistle above the foot pedals
and a scalpel in the pipe to the bellows.
At dinner with Father that very evening,
I begged to première my musical gift.

The country stood still on a chill afternoon.
The radio stations awaited
the opening tones of my generous tribute
to that flat-chested, tuneless coquette.
A diamond drill bit, oscillating, castrated
every last sycophantic buffoon.

In the ballroom my family shivered and sighed
as if pierced by a thin Northern twister.
Then, screwed to their seats, they emitted a scream
that became the new National Anthem.
Blood pelted down the white legs of my sister —
I dug out my earplugs; I dazzled with pride.

The Riddle Ground

Not The Hilton Sisters

Glossy little strumpets
stalk the lawns of spring.
Cookie-cutter beauties,
bottle-blonde, in green stilettos,
they clamour to be seen:
common winnings spat out
from a golden slot machine.

Not A Pregnant Man

My shape
rings true —

an upturned igloo
at a barbeque.

My history's
written in glue,

my cousin
lives in the loo.

My emptiness
has filled you.

Who am I?
Who?

Not Anne Robinson

Nobody touches my bottom!
But my cold embrace is well known.
Endlessly travelling all over the world,
I put pressure on you to go home.

Not As Easy As It Looks

A formal excuse
to peg one's dirty laundry
right to the end of the line.

Beyond all this, enchantment:
a beautiful and measured
way to sound alone.

[Answers in *Notes*]

The Dance
After Paula Rego

It was Sophia's birthday again.
We polished our shoes and washed our hair.
I wore my best yellow skirt —
the one she spat on in the square.

The moon was full as it always was
on that particular night of the year:
they used to say when she was born
lumpy muffs of fat and fur
grizzled from her ears.

No one says that now, of course,
now our tongues are still.
Now she's come into full possession
of the windowless house on the hill.

Even the owls were quiet
the night her mother died.
We stayed at home and locked our doors
so no-one can say they spied
Sophia torch the old red barn
with the horses still inside.

The next day she swept the ashes
off the cliff into the sea,
then she hired the son of the butcher
to scour the earth till it shone.
A charcoal foam churned up the beach,
vomiting shells and bits of bone.

I was her daughter's teacher then,
little Marta's favourite one;
I gave her special lessons in art
until she started to call me 'Mammy'.
Now I count the pencils in the corner shop,
massage my gammy leg.

On Fridays I close early,
battle my way through the geese,
report my quota of thieves
to the milk-faced chief of police

The man I loved was found face down
in a blistered torrent of dung —
no one could tell you the name of the creature
whose arse it had sprung from.
But it was Gregor, Sophia's brother,
who scraped my sweetheart's face
off with the bubbling scum.

I suppose one day she'll simply announce
the date of my marriage to Gregor.
For now she's happy to watch me flinch
when her party brings us together.

Whatever the year, it's always the same:
on the ground where the barn
once whinnied and neighed
an orchestra gathers that day,
rehearsing in silence on stringless violas
and a fishnet timpani drum.

Creeping like twilight up the hill
we shiver in clumps at the gate.
No matter how early or late we arrive
there's always a famishing wait.

I thought I was numb to the marrow,
could limp through the dark in a trance;
but my heart cried out like a nail in my chest
the night little Marta learned how to dance.

I didn't dare speak to the girl:
the Aunts never let her out of their sight.
They taught her the steps of the Crone's Delight
till she screamed like a gull at the moon.

But over Gregor's shoulder I watched her,
as he pressed his groin into mine.
The sweat of his cheek
                    ate into my skin,
and I prayed one day she'd remember

the crayons I gave her,
the kisses, the praise
for her drawings of puppies
and graves.

Monster

i.m. Aileen Wuornos

A prairie girl
at heart, murdering dickheads
was never her dream

as she hitched lifts
on the highway, roller skated at the rink,
girlfriend floating on her arm.

Poverty, psychosis, and a history of incest:
hardly box office bullion,
her all-too-common claim to fame —

but America, I'd queue for hours
to watch once more
the woman being raped in a film

get up, grab a gun,
and blow the fucker
back to Kingdom Come.

A Pint, A Drop Or A Rope

The black comfort
of speaking well of the dead.

Like sipping Guinness,
or chewing liquorice,

half-smiling their names
brings a treacly glow

to the mouth. Your mouth,
that pink hovel

with its one naked bulb
and damp mattress

where no-one
makes love anymore:

the laughter of the dead
foams like brown balloons,

comes to rest upon your lips,
the shadow of a kiss.

Bonjour, Nouvel An

A black moon capsized,
spilling static rain

between the frozen
sheets of sleet
lying around
the glass pyramid
of the Louvre.

I kicked ice
                skittering
across the courtyard.

Inès, later
your small body
dented mine.

Future Tense

Couldn't you tell it was over,
what you called Judgement Day?
Wasn't the future scrawled
on candy pink canvases hanging in banks,
duty-free ads on the road to Damascus,
the ticker-tape swaddling Iraq?
And didn't we drink to the sunset
with cocktails stirred up in a flash:
a slippery surplus of stem cells,
tequila and slush from the poles?
Yes, weren't the animals quiet?
Didn't God jump ship?
Why were you writing poems —
did you think it was 1906?

Midnight Versions of Anna Akhmatova

1.

July 1914

The very air is burnt.
The stench discolours the hills.
Not one sparrow sings.
Even the aspen are still.

The sun is God's furious eye.
It hasn't cried since Easter.
Now He's sent a one-legged beggar
to squat in the yard and yammer:

'The worst is yet to come … the earth
is demanding fresh meat.
There'll be famine, tsunamis, disease,
noon days darker than peat.

'But just as the generals start to carve up
the delicate flesh of your sons,
The Mother of All will spread a white cloth
over the sorrowing land.'

2.

All of us here like a drop and a fuck;
together, we cloud out the night.
On the walls, swallows and roses
stick their beaks in the gathering heat.

You suck that ridiculous pipe,
disappear in contortions of smoke;
I pluck at the hem of my skirt:
my legs are still worth a quick look.

The owner has battened the hatches:
who knows what will fall from the sky?
A cat with electrified fur
bolts out of your beautiful eyes.

Oh God, my heart is sodden
with lager and fear of the bell.
That bitch dancing beside you?
I'll see her later, in hell.

Aphrodite's Answering Machine

Liberties

Shaft of damson in this dress so sheer you hardly wear it. Libertine of a peeling city rakes your breasts with swallow quills.

Clouds above: uncarded goat's wool, snagged on an electrical blue fence. Don't touch the sky. Touch yourself. Note: he likes to watch. Third eye, hood pulled open, takes him in for what he really is. Right foot sliding sweat concavity of collar bone, left heel rests on shoulder, toes strangled in locks of blue-black hair. He crouches down, thrusts up: your knees buckle, the bracken beneath you sings of treason. Practising a Taoist art, he won't ejaculate. Hot mustard seed restrained by a finger you have bitten. Behind the rusting railway tracks, the earth convulses with you both.

He only attends free musical events, most are out of doors. You, for one, are trying to stop taking urban violence so fucking personally. Together you notice far too many anomalies to comment on them all.

His few white hairs grow faster than the rest — the shock that bleached each follicle impels them still. You pluck them one by one with little teeth clenched tight. His pelvis flinches. You cry, an iridescent, deadly spill, because you know you have lived for only this familiarity, the sensations are your identity, and yet it is all too much to ask. *To ask an echo to recall you as dogs fight in the weeds...* His tongue probes your soaking eyelid. He sucks back your toxic tears like escargot. Remember when he washed your feet at dawn, two summers past? What has become of you since then?

Good Definition

cunt (noun) 1. The cunt is the open crossroads of the body, the hot living swamp at the centre of all known directions, the bandits' cave beneath. Pivotal moment that bides its time, eternal source and ever-recurrent destination, the cunt is the volcanic apex of the legs, the unfathomable nadir of the torso, doppelganger of the mouth, internalised breast, throne of emotion, thoroughbred steed of all thoughts. To call the cunt a hole is like confusing the Taj Mahal with an unmarked grave. (Some people can get away with it). The cunt is a funnel of muscle, a meltdown inferno, volatile barometer needle of the body's tropical regions, a runaway train — one long first class carriage — flute of flesh lovingly massaged by a constant column of air. 2. Images of the sweet cunt are so misleading — the elegance, the floral involutions, a glistening delicacy: all lies. The *right cunt* is a death mask buried in the garden, sucking all nutrients out of the soil to keep itself raw. A right cunt is cunning, selfish and, crucially, always gets away with his or her crimes — which, like all crimes, are sublimations of the insatiable desire to be found.

cock (noun) 1. The cock is one handle of a divining rod for subterranean forces — the other is the tongue. The male ego is a crude extension of this sensitive prong, which quivers so rapidly in the presence of its true desire it appears, like a humming bird, to be much larger than it is. The cock is an energy amplifier, a current of flesh. Like a stunning pulse gun with endless rounds of ammunition, or a turret of clay on the wheel, it demands a strong grip — but often the swiftest whisper of pressure will leave it moist and crumpled in its nest. Also comparable to a hot tip at the races, a shaft of light in the catacombs, one rare lily that springs from twin bulbs, at its mightiest the cock is nothing more than a deep, continuous, molecular frisson in the bodies it connects. Nothing less will do. 2. also known as *prick*: a *real prick* is an inflexible stickler, widely open to contempt. Only a real prick dares to boast he can satisfy a *right cunt*, which, by definition (*cunt* 2.) cannot be done. Still, it's extemely *prickish* to raise false hopes.

to define (verb) The process of upending the objection of thought, pouring it into relationships — like shafting infinite space with eternally shifting lines.

Crop Circles

Verve licks my throat while I remember what happens in *The Lover* by Marguerite Duras. 'Look at me,' she spits, knuckling my cleft. Pleasure grows like a cuckoo in a fledging sparrows' nest. *Higher.* The bed veers away from the walls. An untouched jug of water quaking on the floor. With an arm that smells of civet, Verve pins me to the sheet. She knows my name but doesn't use it, preferring 'you', or 'bitch'. If she shuts up for a moment, I'll let her clutch my fanny. And when she's finally forgotten how to speak, I'll hook my legs across her shoulders, crush my squawking beak against her teeth.

Feathering past me, the crow sidles and coughs. Dropped anew each day in strange territory, picked clean of any wisdom or opinions, I know I'll never write a treatise on her blatant harvest of my bones.

Can't you quit talking? Muzzle me with a cage of flesh. Trace appeals to me because her eyes are distorted green glass and her stance is low-slung dangerous, hips fore. Flung into the aviary with the snow owl and the raven, my body edges toward hers. Serious intent. She's not moral but there's no way her cunning can match mine. Oh, but shifting shifting torso friction, chin grinding into breastplate, c'mon Trace. Give unto me your fuck soul, your predatory gristle … I hear her giggle, wriggle free … Verve's thumbs interrupt my tendons. The ones that keep my head on. But can't control my flapping mouth.

Verve's jealous now, lascivious as hell. Now I've got her where I want her, I suppose I ought to crow. 'I'm going to lie on the bed now, Verve, and bend my knee so you can see my pussy glisten. After you fuck it maybe I'll be aroused enough to touch your small wet nose.' Sometimes I start out on my hands and knees and she swiftly fills me up with cock, a smooth wooden strap-on she was given by an artist who only works in oak. Those are the nights I rove over her body, pores stinging, as if her steaming flower could somehow pollinate my face.

I'll say to Trace, 'So. Do you sleep with women?' And if she says no, I'll say 'Oh, I could have sworn you did' and if she says yes I'll say, 'That explains it', because either way I can so easily imagine sliding my hands down her belly, pulling her toward me by her belt. And sure enough, she'll take me home, part my thighs with the point of her leather-tipped riding crop and, with a supple branch, flay my finest hair. I'll bear the welts like extra nipples, try in vain to hide them from the talons of another woman's pride.

The bed's a field of wheat Verve is threshing with her mouth. My clit a smashed-up snail at the centre of the maze. I could pivot round her tongue forever and still she'd fingerpick my shell. We spend hours unweaving shadows of each other, then she'll yawn. At dawn, I have to go.

For Achilleas: Because I Wouldn't Let Him Watch

From the beach on Crete I pick up bulbous pebbles (red), a
prickly urchin (dead), a smiling driftwood fish. My heart's an
overflowing mattress washed up on the shore; her broken
springs and sodden chambers lie, luxurious, abandoned, across
the pitted rocks. It must have hailed here at the dawn of time,
tumours spat out from the burnt volcano nipples of the moon.

Tonight, the moon's a neon Amazon, straining the straps
of a tight black bra. Hidden in her light, I see Amighdalo
approach.

                        Who, dragging
two wrought iron frames across the barren earth, cannot hear
me breathe. She must have untethered them from a fence
around a chicken hut, letting the birds strut free. I watch as she
scrubs the grey shafts with a stiff brush, using her gorgeous
muscles to scour away the droppings and the grime.

Now Jazmin's visible beside her. Arms full of fishing nets, the
silk cord of her father's dressing gown, the black leather belt he
used to beat her with, stitches (plucked from wrists, forearms,
belly), a long blue high wire — all tumbling wordlessly at
Amighdalo's feet.

              "Truss me?" whispers Jazmin, as though she needs to ask.

I witness the slender, phosphorescent girl being made secure.
Then, before my secret eyes Amighdalo, her mouth a baby
shark, pulls those bristling lips apart, suckles Jazmin's salt.
Leans back on her heels.

                    Amighdalo likes to watch
Jazmin's stomach jerk as the number of fingers inside her
increases. Tucking her left thumb between the girl's buttocks,
hoisting Jazmin on her lap, the older woman rocks
night-heat throughout her limbs   extremities   feeding
frenzies   especially face and tits

Jazmin is so riveting and maimed. When she was very small her father dipped her into a bath of battery acid. Because he gripped her by the thong of flesh between her cunt and anus, these regions of her body were spared the numbness of her skin
its ridges   whorls   taut stretches   obliterated
nerves   luminous, distorted   enormous territories   lost
to touching now

Amighdalo would never tire of looking because Amighdalo was amnesiac and every savaged instant was fresh as mother's milk to her. An innocent magician reaching into Jazmin's vagina, pulling out silvery ribbons of pleasure, she gazed as Jazmin screamed, telling her to breathe and fill herself again. If the girl wept or broke she was gathered in a strong embrace. They loved each other. But they could never float far enough away.

A crimson jellyfish trapped in an opaque plastic bag, this too is my heart's desire. Dragged under by the currents, the wake of tankers, ocean liners — the sorry, panicked, tremulous life of me tugs inside a drowning lung.

Not Quite Arrived

'It's like being married when you have a home. God, it's terrible.'

— *Nico*

There are chambers we may enter and those that remain sealed from within. What divides them is sometimes no more than a paper-thin glass wall. In an overlooked corner of a bar in Seoul, I press my cheek, breasts, belly and thighs against such a partition. I don't know why these soft, defenceless regions should be aroused by isolation, but after an aeon has passed I feel my skin begin to flush. And then the glass begin to give. A woman's form. Obscurity. Warm glass. The finest cognac streaming over me. Blue fire.

There are always ragged edges to the shore. You must always step again out of the same river. The flickering wavelets do not understand you. Their tongues are torn, strips of foreign flags. Gritty particles, blown into your eyes by the wind, are washed away by salty drops. Woman, sand, salt, water, foam. The impression left by a monumental sorrow. Raddled senses, erogenous monotones. No stranger to flame, Lady Go Diving, a chain of lakes around her neck.

That night in Seoul I saw a column erected for a cocktail. Sex On The Beach. A pair of ice-tongs is laid astride the thick mouth of a chiselled rock glass, an upturned tulip glass balanced on the tongs. Then on the tulip base a champagne flute is placed. Using a teaspoon with a handle as long as a forgotten ice-queen's sigh, the bartender fills the tall top glass with cherry brandy, crème de menthe, vodka and a splash of cognac. The glass is tilted, thanks to the uneven edges of the tongs. The bartender pours the Hennessy into the Lower East Side and the meniscus rises until it stands above the rim.

I knew a man named Hennessy once. Only Hennessy. Of no fixed race, no fixed gender, he dusted his dark skin with pale pancake powder, tucked his black curls under a black cap,

brushed his lashes with tar and lined his eyes with cigarette
ash. On his lapel he pinned a ring of hair-dye samples.
Locks of magenta, emerald, burgundy, violet and gold, they
looked like fairy horses tails. I invited Hennessy to
Thanksgiving dinner once: he called it 'the turkey birthday',
and talked only of suicide. Hospitality at his squat was
roasted chestnuts by candlelight; he split the skins with a
black thumbnail and prised out the flesh. He was dead
before Christmas, of a heroin overdose.

The bartender douses the glass edifice with vodka, fills his
mouth with brandy and breathes fire over the whole
translucent tower. A beacon of blue flame rises from torrents
of rum, grapefruit, orange and cranberry juice, filling the
rock glass with warm punch and leaving the jewelled flute a
prize for the companion of the one who buys the drink. Sex
On The Beach at US66, Seoul. (Revisited, believe me). The
drink that in my quiet Sunday evening mind morphed into an
image of Nico — elemental siren of frozen foreign lands.

The tulip glass is deeply waisted, a decapitated hourglass on
the bar. Time flows over, not inside it. The sand has long
ago been sucked out by the storm.

The Night Pavilion

Misremembering The Night

Sun squints through the curtains
as I cough into the sheets —
a ball of mousy hair,
my souvenir of sleep.

A fading clot, it squats,
shedding snippets of my voice.
You stir; I sift and worry.
Dawn infiltrates the house.

All I wanted was to lift
a moment to the light,
let it vanish like a bitten thread,
a sip of water down a throat.

But my dream of waking up at last
sticks tight inside the knot.
Your lips a broken comb.
My mouth a baffled cat.

Vanitas
for Paul van Gelder

The cherry red curtain rod
is missing a knob,
your wardrobe
pours from a drawer.

Abandoned self-portraits
face up to the wall,
damp flowers
soften the air,

while high on a shelf
a dead pigeon rests,
eyeless,
smothered in dust.

If I had brushes
I'd forge an Old Master,
scrape fruit
in the heart of the scene:

between the bare sheets
and your lacquered heat
my throat
is a lean nectarine.

Around the smeared edges
of our kisses
and whispers
skin petals settle

like the sag
in a mattress,
velvet dregs
of a lifetime in bed.

Animal, Vegetable, Mineral

With wincing scissors
he trims my chestnut bush,
saving tufts of old growth
for burning on the heath.

When I'm bristling
like a coconut,
he lathers up the shaving brush
on a coin of Fenland soap —

surrounding my mound
with foam,
and scraping his razor
into the scree,

he draws a vulpine muzzle
down upon my lips.
My clit sticks out pink
like a tongue tip

as with my gummy muscles
I grip his index finger:
hungry as a fox cub
nursed by a human mother.

The Ballad of the Broken-Hearted

By a sea the colour of rubies,
    Beneath a sky the colour of sand,
I stagger and stutter over pockmarked rocks,
    Kissing and caressing the land.

Tobacco and spices have rotted away,
    White powder dissolved in the waves;
The diamonds fester in the back of the cave
    And the gold has devoured its slaves.

But we swore a vow if we were ever parted
    By waters deep and dark and poorly charted,
As sure as God is great we'd finish what we started,
    And find the long-lost cure for the broken-hearted.

There's a cross the colour of angels
    On a map the colour of mud.
I struggle and strain to recall the terrain
    That you etched on my mind in your blood.

I see a church up ahead like a splintery tooth,
    Jagged and white in the sun —
I pause and pray to Our Lady above:
    Please Ma'am, let this be the one!

As I gaze down the shore for the sign I was told
    — A tree in the shape of a snake —
A lightning flash skewers the sky
    And the rocks are beginning to quake.

But we swore a vow if we were ever parted
    By waters deep and dark and poorly charted,
As sure as God is great we'd finish what we started,
    And find the long-lost cure for the broken-hearted.

The orphan child,
    The meek and mild,
The jilted bride,
    The suicide,

The father of the murdered boy,
    Your average slice of hoi polloi ...
If we could find that buried box,
    We'd heal them all of love's hot pox.

In a wind the colour of whiskey,
    In a rain the colour of rum,
I soar and search in the shadow of the church
    While my heart it beats like a drum.

The earth opens up by that slithery tree
    And I see you arise from the grave.
I whoop and wail like a démented gale!
    But you ain't intending to wave.

Oh, I fall to my knees and I tear at my hair
    As you wipe your lips with your sleeve.
The bottle in your hand falls to the ground
    And I envy Adam and Eve.

You have jimmy-cracked that crate
    And rotten to yer core
You have seized that sacred nectar –
    You have poured it down your craw.

But we swore a vow if we were ever parted
    By waters deep and dark and poorly charted,
As sure as God is great we'd finish what we started,
    And find the long-lost cure for the broken-hearted.

Cruella Degenerates

Professional lesbians with Italian *Vogue*
demeanour, crimson crocodile kisses
and filigree dragon-jaw smiles: a handful
of long slim bodies in lime green sheaths
lifting ripped bodice mouths up to light.
The haute of these women eats light. A posse.
Teeth stained Exclusive Sunshine, seamed
with nicotine. Concupiscent huntresses, they
stalk the insignificant 'm' madonna who fusses
at a bus stop in the rain. The girl who swings
a silver purse, biting all her nails. Her man
is always working on a car she cannot drive. Pulled
apart by *Elle* and *Marie Claire,* she starts to worry
that her make-up is too garish, makes her
look obscene. She doesn't know it but she needs
to be trussed in torn up silks and velvet, feet
bathed in fragrant waters and blood infused
with Cointreau, lips licked into a glimmer
of her former small diffracted self. Thus
without a murmur, doth the girl fall prey
to five rich coke head vamps. An emerald
sorority of ragged edge refulgence, they sense
she is with child and hiss
white smoke in all her holes.

The Angel of Anarchy
after the bust by Eileen Agar

The night you wrapped my head
in a Wake knot of silk scarves,
clipped chains around my thighs,
pressed your cheek against the feather
inked into my breast —

that night I almost felt your breath
warmly puzzling my flesh.
You could have been a robber,
an artist, or a god. But from your smell
of pepper, mixed with baby mouse,

I sensed that who I was
beneath the mask, and why I stayed
a pinioned herald on your bed,

you were too afraid to ask.

Duet

I shop
You sauté
You chop
I flambé

I bake
You grate
I sweeten
You heaten

I salt
You pepper
I salad
You caper

I pour the juice
You juice the pawpaw
I lobster thermidor
You Roquefort

I marinade
You marmalade
I peel
You wholemeal

I risotto
You gateau
You cappuccino
I marshmallow

You mango
We fandango
& tango

You custard
I pie
I wash
You dry

Natasha
or: *The Ballad of the Lovesick Russian Count*

Baba Yaga told me
if I loved you I must die.
To hear these words from those old lips
I had to give her my eye.

Baba Yaga sucked it
like a granny with an egg,
and when she gave it back to me
I could see as far as July.

I took the train to Moscow
to lay my heart at your feet —
with but three months to live and love
I had to be indiscreet!

I lived on bread and buckwheat.
Drank vodka once a week.
All my roubles I spent on you,
your vanity and deceit.

Oh! Natasha, Natasha, Natasha!
        I graffitied the Kremlin for you
Natasha, Natasha, Natasha!
        I freed all the bears in the zoo
Natasha, Natasha, Natasha...
        I painted Siberia blue.

But with your imperial heart
and your Bolshevik soul,
your Saturday job
as a KGB mole,
your decadent longing
for pure rock and roll,
you saved all your kisses
for that bastard – the Pole!

In May we went out walking,
arm in arm around Red Square;
but when I tried to hold your hand —
it was never there.

In June I took you dancing,
you drank champagne all night!
But when I asked for your address
you called me 'doctrinaire'.

By July I was in torment,
as I knew that I must be...
Baba Yaga sent me a note,
her personal guarantee:

if I remained besotted
I would not last the week.
I burned the note to cinders
in a famous fit of pique.

Oh, Natasha, Natasha, Natasha!
    You take strawberry jam with your tea.
Natasha, Natasha, Natasha!
    You piss on Dostoevsky.
Natasha, Natasha, Natasha...
    Could you ever love me?

For with your imperial heart
and your Bolshevik soul,
your Saturday job
as a KGB mole,
your decadent longing
for pure rock and roll,
you saved all your kisses
for that drunkard – the Pole.

The dog days of the summer
growled into my ear,
'She must be mine this very night,
And *he* must disappear!'

Like a Bolshoi dancer
I tiptoed to his rooms,
armed with just a shovel,
I hid amongst the brooms.

I heard you both approaching,
— you tipsy gypsies, you! —
And with a cry of Russian pride,
down on his head my shovel flew.

Natasha, Natasha, Natasha.
        You cry like a delicate banshee…
Natasha, Natasha, Natasha —
        I have a mansion in pretty Helsinki!
Natasha, Natasha, Natasha…
        Was there never a ghost of a chance
that you could ever love me?

For with your imperial heart,
and your Bolshevik soul,
with your murderous venom,
three times blacker than coal,
with the pistol you plucked
from the belt of the Pole,
through my trembling heart
you blew one final hole.

Miss Dickinson Regrets

Blandishments and tourniquets
won't stem the Surgeon's gash —
I left my Ribcage on the Beach,
my brain Pan in the wash.

My Heart I folded in a cloth,
and placed it in a Basin,
with my Skin I stitched a cloak —
no Sleeves to slip your Ace in.

I left my Flesh so far behind
your Love to forage for...
Now with ancient Teeth I munch
Starry porridge raw.

My face remains in Lockets
you lost inside a drawer.
Be careful turning back your Clocks —
inside their slow, infernal Works

I spat one sharpened Claw.

Boas and Blindfolds

Boas and blindfolds
garland your bed.
my eyes are open
but I've been misled.

No longer invited,
blundering in,
lost in your boudoir
I plunder your gin.

Stockings and sequins
hang on the grate.
I seek the fire
but I've come too late.

Stroking your ashes
and raiding your stash,
I'm just a gatecrasher
left off the latch.
Caught in your updraft
I strike a match ...

Oh, the wild horse has bolted,
leaving all her jewels behind:
love letters, lists of lovers
stained ruby red with wine.

I knew I could not keep you
from the heather in the hills;
I thought I could protect you
from the needles and the pills.

Poppies and seedcake
litter the floor.
I catch a whiff
of the dreams of a whore.

Lost in the fragrance,
I forget vengeance —
deep in my reverie,
I finger your lingerie.

We are embracing,
our bodies are smoke;
yet I am perspiring
under your cloak.

For in the heat of passion
who was rider, who was ridden?
Who bid and who forbidden?
Who forgot to lock the stable door?
And who cried out for more?

Oh the wild horse has bolted,
leaving all her jewels behind:
love letters, lists of lovers
stained ruby red with wine.

I knew I could not keep you
from the heather in the hills;
I thought I could protect you
from your own unrivalled skills.

Boas and blindfolds.
Stockings and sequins.
Poppies and seedcakes.
Ashes and gin.

Your Summer Arm

Was it an odd sort of cricket
climbing my oak dresser? No —
an emerald shield bug, you said,
watching as I tried to slide

a piece of A4 paper
beneath its crooked legs.
When a foot caught, and tore,
I thought we both might cry.

*

Where is grass to comfort that green?
Those sweet, young shoots
I slipped from their sheaths
and chewed with wobbly teeth?

Now, as we curl into bed,
outside in the whistling damp
the husk I dismembered today
begins to decay in the leaves.

*

This whirring of thoughts,
rustle of pages,
mean nothing to you
anymore.

Your breathing is so quiet,
I'd hardly know you were there
if it wasn't for the glowing limb
buried in my hair.

Small Blossoms

When the child hides her finger
in a bowl of blue whales,

a busy road falters,
softens underfoot.

When the peace lily unfurls one leaf
to taste uncertain light,

the woman I never became
begins to play with my hair.

When an unloved day
forgives me,

gladness permeates
my eyelids

and I fall asleep
in a deep seabed,

dream
of swimming slowly

through under-
water wreaths.

Things I'm Cool With Now

Needles, nettles, splinters;
Spinach, spiders, peas.
Lessons, long journeys, winter;
Geese, coffee, bees.

Notes

'The Riddle Ground' answers:
1. Daffodils
2. A bowl
3. The sea
4. Poetry

'The Angel of Anarchy': A Wake knot is the heraldic form of the Carrick Bend, and is often depicted as two intertwined serpents.

'Vanitas': A *vanitas* is a Dutch still life painting tradition, depicting images of sensuality and decay.